99 anonymous confessions

D0796344

hate

family

salvation

loneliness

LOVE

SEX God

heartbreak &

alcoholism.

with michael anthony

anonymoUS beginnings

"What's the worst thing anyone has ever called you and how did that make you feel?" I'd ask that question...and then the uncomfortable silence would ensue. These kids were nervous -- sitting under the hot lights, cameras rolling, a large microphone dangling in front of their face. You see, in March of 2011, I had returned to my Midwest, suburban hometown of Wheeling, Illinois to film an inspirational anti-bullying documentary for local gay teens. My goal was to capture their stories of high school homophobia on film, start a dialogue about LGBTQ equality in the community and ultimately convince bullied gay teens that: "If Michael Anthony could go from a limp-wristed, overweight drama dork with imperfect skin and a pleather fanny pack to a (somewhat) successful and totally fabulous Los Angeles actor/writer/producer/singer/ waiter...then you will too! It gets better!"

These teens wanted to participate; truly, they did. However, the reality of opening up about their secrets and fears on camera proved too overwhelming for most. While a handful of them found the courage to choke out their stories under those hot Hollywood stage lights, most simply sat in silence after I asked my question. I was beginning to realize that a feature-length documentary might not be the best way to reach them.

So instead of asking these kids to open up on film, I began emailing them -- nothing wordy, inspirational or preachy; just a simple question in the subject line: "What is it that bullies you?"

I wasn't sure if they'd respond; however, to my surprise, they did...by the hundreds! And not only were the replies coming from Wheeling's gay teens -- but also from their parents, their siblings, their straight friends and classmates. Some of these letters were pages long; others were only a single word or a poem or a drawing. But one thing they all had in common was an author trying to make sense out of the senseless in their life. These letters were the proof that bullying isn't just a "gay thing." All of us, all ages, all demographics, all races of the rainbow are wrestling with something that leaves us lonely; and ultimately, all we desire is the chance to be heard, to get that pain out of our heart and into the world.

It's been a year since I sent my first email, and I now have thousands of letters from people all over the country. This "anthology of anonymoUS" is a collection of 99 of these confessions. I've published them exactly as received and as written by their author. I keep them anonymous because I truly believe that what bullies us does not define us; we are not the worst thing that anyone has ever called us. We are not that easily broken.

With this collection, it is not my idealistic goal to convince you that "It Gets Better!" Because I am not sure that it always does. Nor with this book am I hoping that you identify with each of these letters -- because some of these confessions are far too unique or extreme to read familiar. My goal in publishing this anthology is that you empathize with these stories, that you take in the emotion behind them -- the guilt, the sadness, the loneliness -- and remember the last time you felt that very same way.

Because when we truly allow ourselves to experience someone else's pain -- when we don't try and convince them "It Gets Better!" but simply sit with them as they try to make sense out of the senseless in their life -- it is only then that we realize how truly connected we are. The things that bully us may be unique, but the scars they leave behind are universal. Even when life leaves us feeling anonymous, we are never alone.

Even in our darkest moments, we are never alone.

www.IAmAnonymous.org

Disappointed

I came here with a guy I like. I was hoping for something to "click" or happen
    It hasn't yet
I want him to kiss me. But I don't think he will
    I got my hopes up too high

I feel sad. Again

I feel like a disappointment
    I cut again yesterday, and the day before
After months of not

I feel like a waste

#606

This drawing represents my family's dirty little secret.

My father is a homosexual.

He didn't bother to tell my mother this until they had already been married for 11 years and my brother and I were born.

My mother thinks having another baby will solve my father's closeted feelings. I think it will just bring another person into this world that wasn't meant to be here in the first place. Like me.

His hands all over me
the room dead silent
I hear his breath on my neck
I smell the beer.

He's my brother
fondling with my body.
I cant stand my flashbacks
he has tore m ore apart.

His hands all over me
the room dead silent
the beer on his breathe
I'm helpless.

Every day that I don't cut my arms, I win. Every day that I eat at least one meal, I win. Every day that I hear "I love you" from someone, I win. For those things didn't used to happen a lot. Being a 17 year old boy, I have almost 100 scars on my arms, legs and shoulders. I starve myself to lose weight and then I binge when I feel bad about myself. This doesn't really help me at all, I mean I am not skinny or fat (I have been told) but that's how I see myself.

Sadly, I can't see the "beauty" that my boyfriend and others see in me. I try, I work my ass off to see myself as beautiful. I don't.

Entitled: "Bullied Daily"

#302

I cannot sleep anymore, and I cannot say why. I used to toss and turn and try to fall asleep. But now I embrace it. I accept that lying awake (while my boyfriend drifts away peacefully) is my lot in life. It's how my nights are to be spent from now on.

There is no use in fighting or trying to reprogram your body. The heart wants what the heart wants, but a sleepless mind is always more powerful than the heart and its wantings.

Have you ever noticed that during the day, the minutes move so quickly...but at night, time moves so very slow? 4:00am to 5:00am is the slowest. It's like the world stops. Everything is silent and calm. It's almost as if I am the last one alive and everything else is dead...or silently dying.

Yet my mind races. It will not stop racing. For that hour, everything seems hopeless. Everything seems to weigh too much. Everything seems to crush my soul, my spirit and my will to succeed.

But then 5:01am comes, and I feel as if a weight is lifted. I feel like a whole different person. I cannot say why. But it always does. This always happens to me each and every night now. I cannot say why.

I dread this hour, and yet I am thankful for it. Because it makes me realize how strong I am for the 23 other hours of the day. I do not understand this, and yet it has become a part of me.

I cannot say why.

I was once a broken boy, full of self-hatred and pity. Why couldn't I be like the other little boys? Why was I always too girly for my father? Why did I need to "man up" for him to love me? Why couldn't he love me? Just me. Who I was, what I liked, and everything else. Why was I a disappointment to him? Should I just give up? My mother had. She left two years ago. When I needed her mostly on my death bed, self-induced of course, I still needed her. I always will. What is a boy without his mother?!? Half-complete and unwanted. That's where I was. I still grapple with it. How can I get close to someone if they leave? I want someone to love me like she was supposed to, love me fully like my father was supposed to. How can I get a man who will love me like I need? Like I want. I worked my ass off in sports, in school, and at work. Maybe then he will love me? Maybe I will get what I need from my father. The ONE person who is still there.... for now. My boyfriends give me so much yet, it's never enough. I leave the relationship hoping, "maybe the next one won't cheat, or he can love me for more than my body or. maybe he can actually say that he really loves me?". Too many "maybes" and not enough "for sure's" Should I wait? Should I move forward? Does sex mean he loves me? If I get drunk, will I be free enough for him? If I get high, will he love me then? Will I ever really know? Hello? HELLO—? Fuck this, I can't take the pain any longer. maybe someone else can love me?

Signed,

A Questioning Gay Boy. ♡

#303

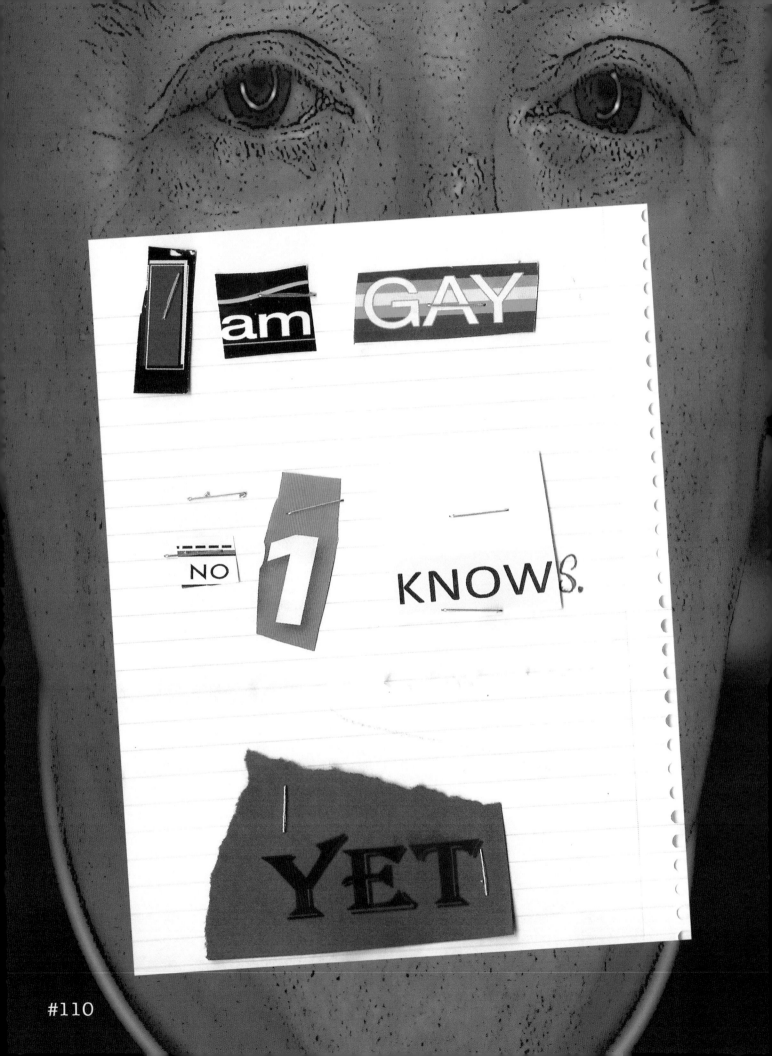

I am 31
I've never been
kissed

and nobody
knows

#108

waking up in the morning, looking at myself in the mirror! Your fat, your ugly. I know that thur Joking around, but how do you think it makes me feel?
Even walking in the high hallways of school I can hear it STOP STOP it! Its NOT Funny... ———▷ Insecurity lonliness
                                    Sadness

I feel used, like thats all he wanted from me SEX. After that its like I am some other gurl that had sex with him. Now I felt filthy and disgusted. Knowing that, that was all you wanted makes me fee like a no1 like I am trash. I should of known from the first time I talked to you. what's your problem. LEAVE ME ALONE.

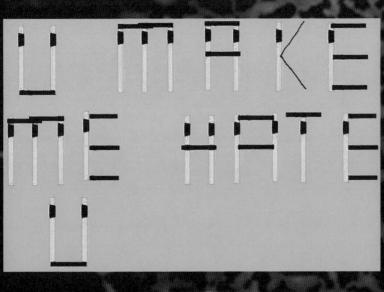

I hate my body.
I hate my job.
I hate my boss.
I hate my life.
I hate myself.

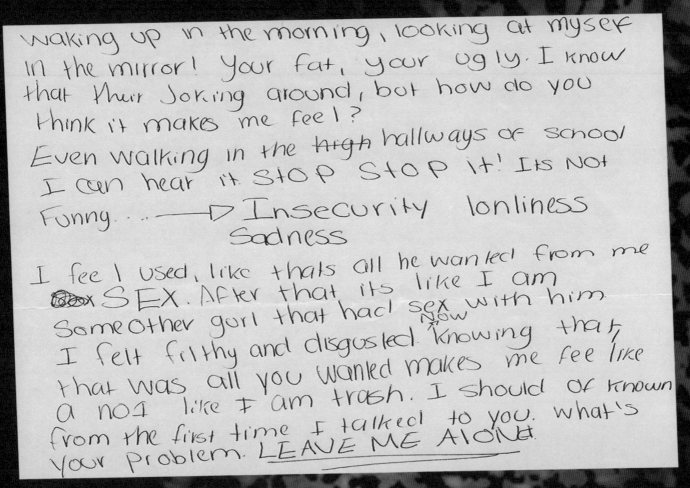

Entitled: "13 & Broken"

#620-#623

My son is 16 and has "come out." He says he is gay. Personally I do not understand how someone can KNOW they are gay at such a young age, but I respect his feelings and path in life.

Despite what my friends have incinuated, I see nothing wrong with my son's choice. (Is it a choice? Who knows what to believe anymore. Science, JUST TELL US ALREADY!) He is who he is and he is happier than he's ever been since this "coming out.".

If he ends up being gay, not a single part of me minds in the least. I wish him love and happiness, much more of those two emotions then I have ever experienced.

What I DO have a problem with is that he's grown lazy like a sloth. His As have turned into low Bs. He says he's too busy to hold down a job, yet shows nothing accomplished with his free time. He's gaining weight.

It's not depression. I've asked him a million times. He's just getting fat and happy. Simple as that. I am sorry, but no 16 year old should be THAT content yet. Do you want to live in your parent's house for the rest of your life, SON?
I should hope not! Plan for a future and get your act together, SON! Get on a tredmill and put down the chip bag! (Oh that made me laugh!)

Be gay. Who cares. but just remember that doesn't give you a life or a personality. Get a job and get with the program of life. I won't be able to take care of you forever, and I wouldn't want to either. Mommy is trying to get her own life together, and that starts today!!!

(I re-wrote this three times to erase any hint of who he'd or I might be! I would DIE if he knew I really felt this way! But I do!! Fat and happy and all!!!)

This morning I woke up, rolled out of bed and drug myself to the coffee pot.

A 9:15am start time isn't late, but everyone in my life makes me feel as if I'm on a 24/7 holiday, like I do nothing but go out to lunch and get my hair done.

I am a homemaker who no longer has a home. (We recently downsized from a 2-floor to a condo when my last children went to college. Finally!) There's no more driving my babies around town, supporting them at local sporting events or any other "mom" stuff. All that "mom" stuff that used to take up so much of my day is over.

I remember all the other moms and I, when we'd be waiting at some basketball game or in some carpool lane, would be talking about how our lives would change once the last kid left. How we would get executive jobs with our kid-tested and mother-approved skills. How we would take over the world. Or at least travel the world.

But then the kids leave. The basketball games and carpools stop. These women (and unemployed men) that you saw day in and day out, you just stop seeing. They make no effort to contact you, but you make no effort to contact them. It's like that 22 years of your life never happened.

I get up at 9:15am every day, but I could get up at noon. No one would notice. I used to think that would be freedom. Now I realize that it's limbo. It's purgatory for a "former" parent.

I miss my babies!

From the Artist: "It's called 'Our New Family.' I drew this after my Daddy died...That's me in the front and that's my Mommy sad. We both miss him every day. He was sick. He was my best friend...My name is Henry. I am 4-years-old."

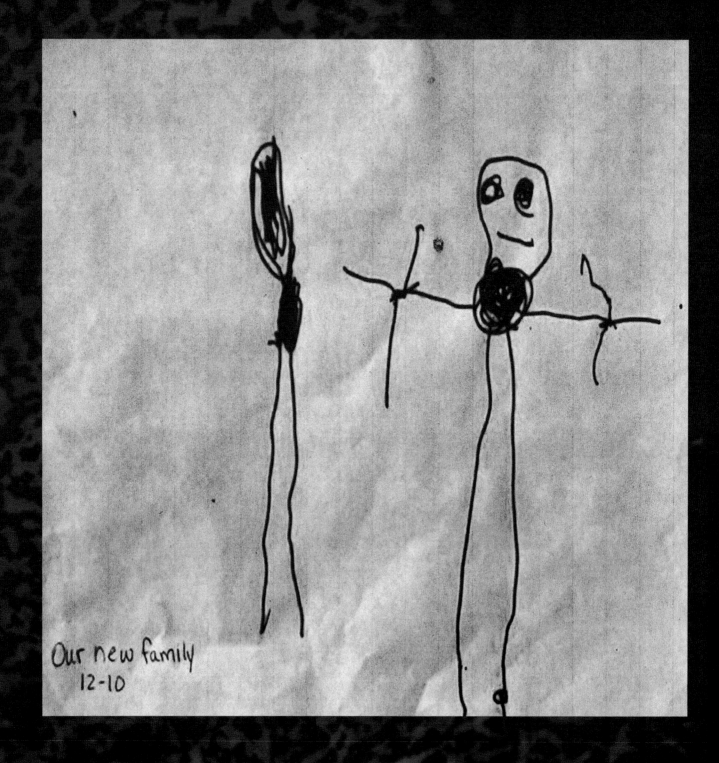

Our new family
12-10

From the photographer: "This is a photograph I took of my son, Henry, napping in Tulum, Mexico. This was our first vacation together after my husband Leo died of cancer. He was 36 years old...This photo makes me smile and cry at the same time. It's pure magic...because some days it feels like love is worth it and some days it hurts so goddamn much. For me, this photograph is the proof that in the end, love is worth it."

Nothing

I see nothing
I feel nothing
I do nothing
I say nothing
Meaning, i am nothing in
this world.
I make a noise,
mumbling the english
language
but no one sees me
No one hears me
I add more sound waves
into the echo of the
drizzling
rain
on my window pane
But
i am nothing more
I am a spec of dirt on this
earth compared to
the universe.

Another person trying to
fight for life
I blend in.
I blend into the crowd
I am another color in the
mash up of human
beings around me
I seem like nothing.

Invisible is what they call it
I could be sitting on the side of the
street
Begging for money
But the buissness boys and city girls
would
walk
right
past
me
As if I blend
In
The
Crowd.
I am nothing
I lay here on my bed,
listening to my heart
beat

The rain taps my window
As i lay here i think
My heart means nothing.
Ive lost my soul
And all my hope.

I am nothing in this world.
I wouldnt be noticed if my body
disappeared

The world would still spin.
It wouldnt explode or cause a
earthquake
I would just be another life lost in
2011 Nothing.
My name would be written in books.
But, those letters would mean
nothing
After the world moves on.

I see nothing
I feel nothing
I do nothing
I say nothing
Meaning i am nothing..

But, how do i become something?

#550

I am angry
I am upset
I am alone
I am left out
I am in high School
I am a girl
I am outgoing
I am social
I am sad
I need someone
anyone
    who will be there
    not just friends
    who know me
    but a mother
    who understands
    me. For who
      I am.

#600

If the world knew the truth, it would stop and stone me. There would be pandemonium in the streets. People would search rabidly for me. Their only goal would be to kill the dirty inside me. I see this daily. I see people staring at me and silently praying for my soul. They have given me two options. Change or disappear. I am young and they believe there is still hope for me. This judgement is palpable. I sit in this coffee shop and feel it all around me. The teenage girls with their jock boyfriends at the corner table. The college drop out working behind the counter. Even that old woman in the overstuffed chair reading a romance novel. In their eyes, I am on my last leg. I am on the verge. I can either turn around and run into the arms of their salvation or I can jump of this cliff into the sinful unknown.

Today, I bought a bus ticket to San Diego. Today, I jumped.

In 2005, my goal was to move to LA.
In 2006, my goal was to pay my rent in LA.
In 2007, my goal was to get famous.
In 2008, my goal was to be sexy and popular and wild and carefree and interesting and muscular and all the things I never was in high school.
In 2009, my goal was to get off drugs.
In 2010, my goal was still to get off drugs.
In 2011, my goal was to look in the mirror and not hate the reflection staring back at me. I have succeeded and 2011 has been the best year of my life.
Your demons aren't as strong as you think.
Don't give up.

"10 years AGO...
I shot DRUGS in HERE...
NOW IM CLEAN"

From the photographer: "I took this photo in the bathroom stall of a higher-end coffee shop in San Francisco. Me too was in this stall to shoot it up. Tar black. Negra gold...! I saw this scribbling just after an injection and right before I disappeared from the world. It touched me, so I snapped a shot with my over-priced iPhone...Since then I have not touched anything mind-altering and I think I may be on the path to some sort of sobriety. Perhaps for good. We shall see...Funny how one man's graffiti is another man's salvation. Ugly inspiration! Scar and mar the world I say because your pain is a lesson learned to someone at rock bottom...Thank you to whoever wrote this. I hope you are still clean. And if you are not, please know you are beautiful...Thank you."

#903

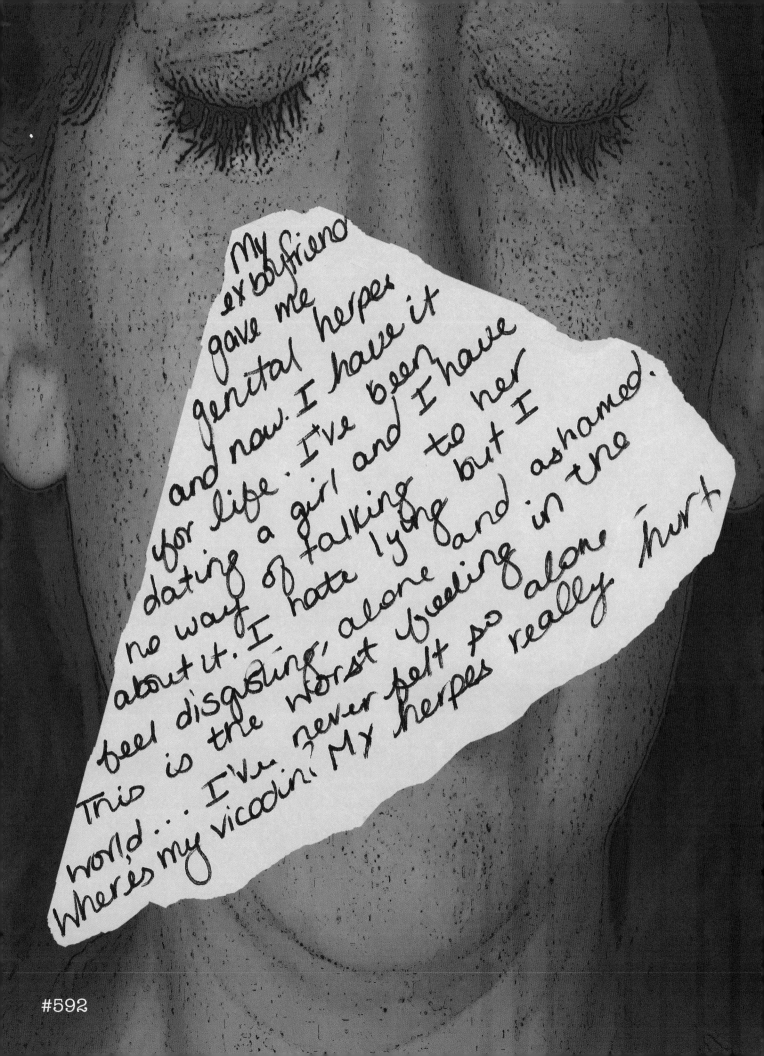

#592

i am just gonna say it
it KILLS me inside so deeply when no one else sees
this

but it's when my parents CUT ME down
embarrass me
tell me that my life will never be full and complete
and "legal"

i understand that they are just being truthful with
their thoughts
i always asked that above all they stay honest with
me

but this is how they feel about a gay son
they already know who i am and all about what i
want to do with boyz!!!!!

but they say it every day
in front of my brother, sister, my friends
and none of them seem to pick up on how much this
KILLS me

i STRUGGLE to be the best version of myself that i
can be
i don't want to be illegal
but i feel i never will be complete or live a full
life

and my parents seem to agree
and since mother is always right, i guess it's true

i now know that it's true

GOODBYE, my LOVE. sometimes love just AINT ENOUGH.

#801

How do I feel right now?

It is early. Early for me, anyway. The traffic is going by outside. It is a
grey day and people are whizzing by in the flow of going hither and thither, I
would assume, to work. I don't have a job. This day has no structure for
me. I am terrified. I have been out of work for a long, long time. I don't
know what I'm doing anymore. Things have not worked out the way I
thought they would. I threw all my savings at buying time...and now it feels
like I'm running out of both. I know that G-d is my refuge. I know that G-d
is my salvation. I know that this will all pass and five years from now I'll
look back on this and think, "Gee, what valuable lessons I learned during
that time of utter financial hell." But today, right now, I feel a panic in my
chest and a lump in my throat because I just don't know what to do. The
blank page scares me. It reminds me of my life. I'm not coming up with
much to fill it. I feel like a failure. A fool. Invisible and precariously self-
placed on the edge of the universe. What's left for me? A job at the grocery
store? Waiting tables? Prostitution? I can't think straight. Sometimes I
just meander from place to place in my apartment literally walking in circles.
The world seems so big and Hollywood feels like constantly trying to push a
huge rock up a hill with no end in sight. Man, I want to pay my credit cards
off. I want to pay off my student loan. I want to know I'll have the rent for
February. I want to know my boyfriend isn't going to leave me because I'm
falling apart right now. I want to know that my book will find a publisher. I
want to know that I can write that screenplay. I want to know that this all
does even out somehow and that the insanity that is the way this world
functions does somehow even out in the end. I can't focus on the negative.
That doesn't help anyone. Still, I want to scream and cry and beat my fists
into the ground until someone takes pity on me and gives me a good paying
job. I feel like a fool. I feel like such a fool. Why the fuck did I ever get
into motherfucking show business? I have NOTHING to show for it.
Nothing. I thought by now I'd have a house and money in the bank and all
the STUFF you're supposed to have. I don't care about stuff, I really don't.
I'm at rock bottom and I want to find that strength within that says, "Yes
you can. This is who you are. This is who we are. Pick yourself up and
keep going. There is a reason to." It gets better? It gets better?!
Sometimes I laugh at this "It gets better" thing that's going on. Sure, it
gets better in terms of being gay and accepting that...but that's NOTHING
kids. It gets worse in so many ~~ways~~ ways. You have to get out into the world and
pay for shit. You have to work doing stuff you never, ever wanted to do.
You have to answer to assholes. You have to pay off your debts. You have
to keep going in a world that makes no sense at all half the time. None.
And you have to be strong and adult and blah blah blah. Hell, I wish I had
someone paying for the roof over my head and buying me clothes and
making sure I ate and stuff like that.

Still, somewhere in Palestine, a little girl just wants a drink of fresh water.
At least I can go to my fridge and take care of that.

G-d, please guide me. I need more help than I've ever needed in my life.

I decided to follow my dreams and (as the past 6 months have shown) that was a total mistake. You watch television or you listen to inspirational speakers, and you always get the message that dreams are meant to be followed. But what we seem to forget is that those television shows are fake, over-produced breaks from reality and that those speakers are multi-billionaires with not a care in the world.

I left a job I have been at for 3 years. A job that gave me benefits, good pay and (more importantly) a place to be in the morning. Now I find myself walking the halls of my apartment. (Well, walking the hall. "Halls" makes it sound as if I have some mansion or something. I do not. I have a 1-bedroom apartment in Silverlake that's approximately 800-square-feet with exactly one hall that is about 3 feet long.) To say that I walk this hall all day would be dramatic.

But I am dramatic.

I guess the tragic part is that if someone asked me, I couldn't tell them what my dream was anymore. It used to be this esoteric kind of thing. I wanted to be an "artist at large". I didn't want to be tied down by labels like "poet", "actress", "writer" or "dancer". I wanted to be that woman who had it all. At least artistically speaking.

But that's not how LA works. You find one thing you're good at, push forth and pray to GOD that it works out. You hope that eventually someone WILL label you a "poet", "actress", "writer" or "dancer". You yearn for success of some sort. You hope for a place in the world, one that actually pays you and maybe even pays you well to do what you love. I do not have that. I may never have that.

Time to go walk the halls. I mean, hall.

My grandpa got *really* fucking drunk last night like you wouldn't believe. I find it disappointing because he's been so good lately. He's been a good example for me and he's been showing everyone that he's really trying, but I don't blame him. Last night fucking sucked. Maybe was even the worst night of my life. No I *know* it was the worst night of my life.

Part of me blames Marissa my oldest sister but none of this is her fault. It never was and never will be her fault, but it's easy to blame her. I can't blame her for what happened, but I can blame her for how she's been dealing with all of this.

I'd better explain it all upfront . I keep trying to talk about the story and getting it off my chest without telling the story but no one understands what I'm saying. The truth is really simple though. Tragedy is always simple. My sister was pregnant. She went into labor. She was a mother, but only for like 2 days and then her baby died. When the baby was inside her, everything seemed fine (even with all of the tests), but it wasn't fine. There was a heart ventricle problem that affected the blood pumping.

My mother has told me twice that I'm too dumb to understand the exact details, but I know it's only because she's upset and SHE doesn't understand it. I'm not dumb, I'm just a good punching bag for my mom when shit like this happens. (I am also very smart. I am a bad writer as you can probably tell, but when it comes down to it I'm actually smart, and a really good punching bag too!)

Anyhow, My sister asked me to be a godmother 6 months ago. Well she invited me to be a godmother, but she also told me that she wouldn't have a godmother for her baby who was doing drugs or drinking or failing *any* class (especially espanol!) or is not going to church. As dumb as it sounds all it took was her asking and I got on the ball. In less than 2 months I stopped being a dumb ass and got things together. I even lost like 12 lbs!

(I still failed gym class but once your failing it's kind of hard to get out of that hole, which is stupid because it's GYM CLASS but I am taking two gym classes the end of my senior year to make up for it and it will all be fixed, but that has nothing to do with what happened or why I'm writing this.)

I was a godmother, but only like for 2 days.

Why did my sister choose me? My younger sister Patricia is too young to be a godmother and my mom is the grandmother and my aunt became Jewish (!!!!!) with her second husband so I seemed like the best choice. Maybe the only choice, but when I made changes in my life, I WAS the best choice. Then the baby came and the baby died and none of us saw it coming. Not even God (well, if god did see it coming, he didn't tell the GODmother.) (And even if he did see it coming and told me, I wonder if I would have told anyone. Actually, maybe God did know but was just unwilling to tell me. A truly loving God would never put someone, not even a Godmother, in the position of having to share news like that, rite??)

1

My sister was going to name my goddaughter Sofia. One, because it's pretty. Two, because it's a modern take on our great-grandmother's name Sophia. Three (which she doesn't say but my brother in law Tommy has said jokingly more than once), because Sofia was in all honestly most likely conceived on a sofa! (He's classy like that. No though, don't judge him, it's really funny when he says it, and true I'm guessing.)

Anyhow, what I CAN blame my sister for is not my goddaughter dying but my sister refuses to acknowledge that Sofia was a person. She was here with us for two days. She cried and her hands moved and she watched me. I would make these dumb faces and the baby would smile. Everyone says it's gas, but it looked like a bunch of smiles to me and that's all that matters. (Maybe all smiles are gas??? Think about it.)

Well, My sister refuses to give the baby her name. SOFIA! My sister refuses to talk about anything. She sits in the living room on the couch and watches TV all day. She talks on the phone to Rita and Janel and they laugh like nothing every happened about the dumbest shit all day long. Then every night the entire family gets together. We all sit on the porch and cry. My uncle, stepdad and grandfather (now as of last night) drink a lot. (Don't worry, I don't drink anything.) We all talk about Sofia and what might have been and we cry. My grandpa wails. (It was his mother who was named Sophia.)

My sister does not come outside. She only bangs on the window once in a while which is her way of telling us to shut the fuck up. My mother is horrified saying my sister doesn't care and is a monster, but you should hear the way my sister bangs on the window. It's violent and loud like the world is exploding in our living room. The way she hits the glass is like a bomb has gone off in the middle of our house. (but maybe it has, rite???)

What do I want right now? I want my sister to stop laughing on the phone. I want her to acknowledge how we are feeling but also how she is feeling. I want her to stop saying THE baby and I want her to start saying SOFIA at least once in a while. Because when (if!) she uses Sofia's name, it'll make it more real for all of us. I think it will open my sisters eyes. I think (I hope) it will bring her to her knees and she'll start to wail like my grandpa does.

Because it's not until my sister has her breakdown that I feel I have a right to have my breakdown. I made a vow to guide Sofia to God and now Sofia is with God, but my job is not done until I also bring peace to her mother, my older sister, my best friend.

and then I can finally have MY breakdown. I need to breakdown too. Soon.

(Please do not change any of these names I've used in my letter. This is my family. This is our life. This is our story. This may be the last time anyone writes about Sofia and I want this published, I want it read and I want it to inspire people to get up off the couch and love everyone everyday. Thank you.)

The scar on my arm is a physical manifestation of hate.

Only 3 people in my life know how it got there.

Only 1 other person has ever been courageous enough to ask.

I did not tell him.

It's not that I was embarrassed to tell him.

I did not tell him because the story is filled with hate and ugliness.

I refuse to retell it to anyone.

I refuse to put that energy back into the world.

My silence has made the world a better place.

All that remains of that incident is a scar on my arm, and I can deal with that.

Silence can be golden.

To you, this may look like a broken ruler.

To me, it is more. Much more.

It is a bookmark.

As a child, I accidentally broke this ruler. Crying, I gave it to my Grandmother and asked her to fix it.

She said, "I cannot fix it. It is broken and now has no use as a ruler. However, it has other uses."

She took one half and then gave me the other. "This is no longer a ruler," she said. "It is a bookmark. Two bookmarks, in fact. One for me and the other for you. Sometimes separately and other times together, we will read and then we will grow."

We read. We grew.

I have not purchased a book in four years.

Instead, I have a computer and an iSomething device that reads to me.

I have no use for books, hardcover or otherwise.

I have no use for this bookmark.

With modern technology, I am able to read twice as much twice as fast, and yet I feel I have grown half as much.

You look at this and see a broken ruler. I now see the same thing.

I miss you, Grandma.

#319

My dad is my hero and in one month he might be going to jail. My dad, who taught me all about good music, took us on vacations, gave me all he could. I don't know what to think in the chaos. Or how to help from afar. How to comfort my Mom. He's going to miss the summer, the fall which he loves, family weddings; maybe seeing me in a play. But he says it's gonna be okay. He's comforting my mom. He wants to write a book. He's still my hero. Guess we'll take it as it comes...

#500

10 years ago (and since then) I could not say or do anything. Guilt had destroyed me and All of my emotions stayed locked inside. Then one day I broke open.You can only hold self-hatred inside for so long before it runneth over and you explode.

On Christmas Eve of 2010 I exploded for no reason in particular and since then I have not been able to stop sharing my story.

On October 17, 2001 my daughter committed suicide. (That is not the exact date. I would rather people not know who I or she is, but it was around that time and you get the idea.) My daughter was a lesbian. She never told me this but I always knew this. I cannot explain how this is but it is true. A mother knows. A mother always knows.

Maybe that is why I treated her with so much contempt as she grew up? Some mothers fall apart when they discover their children are gay because they feel like they've lost the dream of a big wedding, being grandparents or something of that sort. I never have had these dreams. I always knew my Becky (my only child and not her real name) was a lesbian. I had trouble connecting with her, not because she was not a loving child because she was, but because I only pictured a future where she lived as a gay woman and me as her straight mother. The two of us would have nothing in common. Why foster a relationship with a child you will never really connect with?

I was never abusive or wicked. But I was never there and I made it very clear that I would never be there until she 'softened up'. (I used that term once and everyone in the room knew exactly what I meant. It embarrassed her very much at the time but looking back on it, I should have been the one to be embarrassed.)

Sometimes you stare at your child and wonder why you can't hold her. You want to, but you don't because I don't know maybe you are scared? After this realization, you hate yourself because you wonder 'How can a mother be strong enough to give natural birth to a 9pound baby but not be strong enough to touch her when she's 10years old because of what she may or may not be a decade from then!!'

Becky died in her bedroom when I was at work. When my daughter committed suicide, I was not there. Why? It was not because she was bullied or abused by my lack of good parenting. It was because she fell in love with a girl and was scared. (This we later read in her diary.) It was loving too much that killed my daughter. She learned to love somehow, but I never showed her how to do that. I am forever thankful to whoever taught her how to do that.

Until last December I allowed this to shape me, my life and my future. Then on Christmas Eve for no reason at all, I felt light like a weight had lifted. (I always laugh about this feeling because I originally thought that I was having a stroke!) I began to float like I was out of my body and I've remained in that place since then. I am filled with a strange love and calmness now.

How to explain it? I want to hug strangers on the street. I cry (in a good way) each time someone looks me in the eyes. I feel connected to everything and everyone now. It does overwhelm me at times. However this is the grace I have been praying for. This must be what Heaven feels like.

Is this the type of love my daughter felt? I can understand how it would overwhelm a 15year old girl to death with her not having a mother to talk to. No one taught me how to love in this newfound way, but one day it simply invaded my body and has yet to dissipate.

I learned sadness, regret, and heartbreak from my daughter's suicide. But I feel she has now forgiven me and passed on the gift of love. She has forgiven me. She is teaching me and she will guide me until I join her again. When I do I will never leave her side.

Thank you for listening to my story. I love you.

#009

i'll never be as smart as him. no matter how hard i try. i'll never be as athletic as him. no matter how hard i work at it. i'll never be as funny as him, it just won't happen. i know i should love him, being my big brother + all. But how can you love the thing that you are being compaired to all day, everyday. "Why can't you be more like him?" is all i hear. i know i do love him, i just don't love all his success.

I ♡ you brother!

My dog.
I miss his furry ADORABLE face.
Always careless.
always free.

HE MADE ME
ME!!

Entitled: "A Family Turned Upside-Down!"

Oh no I am not anonyymous anymore

no, i will not be ever again

i will fight for your life

even though you did not fight for your own

your 6 brothers and sisters and I have lost our hearts

by losing you

i did not sign up for this

u were 16

u will always be 16 now

too young, too beautiful

when we found you

swinging

I want to snort again................HOPELES

SNESS AND EMTINESS ARE FEELINGS MADE BY YOUR OWN
CHOSING. I SAY SIT ON IT AND FUCKING SPIN ASSHOLES. I
LOOOOOOOOOOOOOOOOOOOOOOOOOO

OVE THE RUSH.

I MADE A CHOICE TO HAVE IT IN ME—without or with those
that agree with MY CHOICES. It all flows from within me, FOR
living without it is just a mere shell of existence--albeit a very
persistent one, that the better half of me

De
sires.

Entitled: "Where I Go
When I'm High..."

Entitled: "Every Night Until I Get a Job!"

Evil is subversive. Calling someone faggot or cunt is not acceptable. It will get you slapped in your tracks by the Politically Correct powers that be. If you call someone one of those words, society will rip your head off and spit down your neck. Kids know that and they're not stupid.

Bullying is less obvious now. It's not done out in public with words or weapons. It's done on the sly. It's a look. It's a giggle. It's complete apathy. A teacher cannot yell at a student for staring or giggling or not caring, but those actions cut just as deep.

There's this bitch that calls my BRYAN which is short for BRYANT which is short for LANE BRYANT which is obviously a fucked up crack at my weight. Yea, I'm a fat ass. I'm huge. I look at myself and I see a disgusting beast. But where the fuck did this bitch get this idea that she had the right to throw this in my face every day? It's my own personal battle, and it has nothing to do with her.

She walks down the hall and pretends to cough and calls me BRYAN under her breath. I don't fight back. I've done what I'm told. I've "reported" it to "the authorities" (my teachers.) I've explained the situation and what she means by it. They all tell me that I must be imagining it or "that's not what she means",

How the fuck would you know, "Ms. Authority" who weights about 110 pounds???? You haven't walked a day in my fat bitch shoes. I see my nickname for what it is. It's a heartless cut at my weight. I know you see it too, or you can at least imagine that there is some truth in my complaint.

If you take me seriously though, then you have to do something about it. She's a beautiful honor student with an important mom and a beautiful smile. I'm a fat piece of shit with a dead father and a D-average and a pregnant sister. (I can't even afford something from Lane Bryant. OH, the IRONY becomes evident as I cackle at this!)

I go ignored, and I'd like to say that you go ignorant but you don't. You go apathetic and like I've said at the beginning of this ramble, apathy is subversive evil. You're part of the problem as much as she is, and your smile isn't nears as beautiful as hers.

I lay in bed listening to the mechanical sound of the bathroom fan and the sound of my cats sleeping - cats snore - how weird is that?

I can't sleep because I am in constant pain. My back, my neck, the migraines and the ringing in my ears. A day doesn't go by that I don't think about ending it. There's pills (I have so many for my pain) or the razors in my art box (all fresh and sharp).

It is almost impossible for someone that doesn't exist in the pain, real, physically debilitating, pain, to understand what I am going through.

So I lay in bed, listening to the world pass me by, because I am in too much pain to participate in it anymore. I take a bad handful of pain pills to leave the house, including tonight, and I bite back the tears when the pain starts to take over again.

When I look in the mirror (which I try not to do), all I see is a fat cripple that no one would want to love. No one would want to get involved with someone that needs a wheelchair to walk further than the couch. No one would want to touch someone this fat and broken. So why bother, right? I'll never have my dreams come true and I'll never have someone that loves me AS I am -

So I look at the pills and the razors, and I tell myself, maybe tomorrow won't be as bad.
                                    - Me. -

High school is for idiots. Am I the only one who understands this? It is a natural evil, I suppose. It is something our society forces us into thinking that children need. Not so.

Think of everyone rich you know either professionally, personally or via the news. What are they for doing? Opening a business or discovering something new that people NEED. I am sure. It is always something creative. Yes it may be something science-based or technical, but we learn none of these things in school anymore.

High school is about meeting requirements and making the GRADE = A+. Mostly, it is about test scores, funding and teacher's getting their precious tenure. This is true. We all know it. Why won't someone just say it?

WHAT OTHER business do you know that has a tenure aside from teaching? Supposedly teachers are the gateway to the future and mold our youth, but most get lazy and will never lose their jobs. They are sucking your tax dollars and taking expensive vacations during their PAID three-weeks off!.

No person that ever got rich on their own successful company allowed their employees to get tenure, I am sure. Am I right? Think about it.

If a student fails just 2 tests in honors physics, he drops to regular physics. If he has trouble with that, he loses the ability to stay in the honors track at all. This affects his college aps which affects his college acceptance which affect his future.

Maybe he's just an idiot when it comes to physics, but maybe he's a genius when it comes to English, football or saving lives. Because his physics scores suck, he's ruined your state wide test score average so you've ruined his life through the college application process. (DON'T EVEN GET ME STARTED ON THAT ONE! $75 a pop. I think NOT!)

One of 2 things is happening here. Either I'm the only one telling the truth, or I am bitter at 17. I am bitter, but I am also telling the truth.

Thank you for ruining my life and see you in community college if I am even inspired enough to go anymore. E=mc=you're an idiot= the joke must be on ME.

When I was a lot younger than today I used to be a lot fatter in everyway. Theatre was about all I did from age 8 on. It was the only place I thought I belonged. Then one day in the dressing room in front of all my friends I assumed. It was declared by one I needed a bra, to cover up the tits that he saw. As I quickly tried to cover my upper half I stood there and watched everyone laugh. Never in my life had I felt this kind of shame and to my defense not one 'friend' came. Looking back on this now it amazes me how peoples own fears gave them a silent vow. Now I live in LA and as a personal trainer help others everyday escape this fate. To me they turn to open the gate. It's not about what happens to you and this is so true — it's about taking that lesson and doing what you do.

it has been 14 hours since my last drink. Before that, I had gone a week. before that, I went a couple of days.

I black out often now. nightly usually now. I've hit my girlfriend when blacked out. I've pissed myself when blacked out. I've shit myself when i've been blacked out.

But I don't stop drinking. I say its because I don't want to stop. But deep inside I know it's because I cant stop. I've never said this outloud. But I've written this down many times. In the journal I've started keeping. They say admitting it is the first step.

I've admitted it on paper. Does that count?

Since I keep pissing and shitting myself, I doubt it does.

I ask god for salvation when no one is looking and no one is listening. Nightly now. And especially at seven PM when I get home and reach for the vodka and mix a drink before even putting down my gym bag

But god doesn't save me. I know he cares for me. I know I am loved by him. I know he has a plan for me and this will one day end. I will soon learn a lesson

that terrifies me. I drive drunk almost daily now. Do I have to kill someone to learn the lesson im supposed to learn. I hit my girlfriend, not nightly actually only on a few occasions ever. But do I have to scar her on the inside or on the outside to learn my lesson? Do I have to lose my job, lose my family, or lose my friends to learn this lesson?

God, I wish u could climb inside me and erase this evil before you (or probably before i) lose everything. I am told that I was made in your image. Then, I have a question for you…

do u shit yourself when you black out?

#057

~~[scribbled out lines]~~

I've hid behind all of the things that have happened ~~so~~ in my life. My family lost three members in 2 weeks. Big whoop. My parents divorced. How ORIGINAL. People pretended to like me, but "secretly" told everyone how much they hated me. Cliché.

I don't really know how to ~~so~~ transition here, so....

~~[scribbled out]~~ I have a lot of secrets, and they've mostly only been hidden from ~~my~~ my family. One: when I was 19, I was raped. I still think I "had it coming." Two: When I was 13 (ish) I stole my dad's credit card to look @ lesbian porn. I got confused & gave up. Three: I've known I "wasn't straight" since I was 10, but my family won't ~~a~~ accept it... so I haven't told them. My brother calls me a dyke constantly (as a joke), but he'll never understand how much it kills me when I don't reply, "And if I am?" Four: My best friend died of cancer. I knew about the ~~tumor~~ lump, but I ~~o~~ didn't do anything about it, like tell her to go to the doctor. ~~Her~~ Her 21st birthday would have been this past Wednesday. (I didn't go to work.) Five: I say I'm a stronger person than I was before, but I doubt it. I fall apart every day.

I'm finally a writer, but I hate what I write. I disagree with the "angle" my editors force on everything.

I love my friends... I think. I don't know what love feels like. Thats NOT an exaggeration. I don't know it, and don't understand it. I think I love everyone, but thats ridiculous. I don't have a reason for my life, and it kills me to say that, and to know its true.

#572

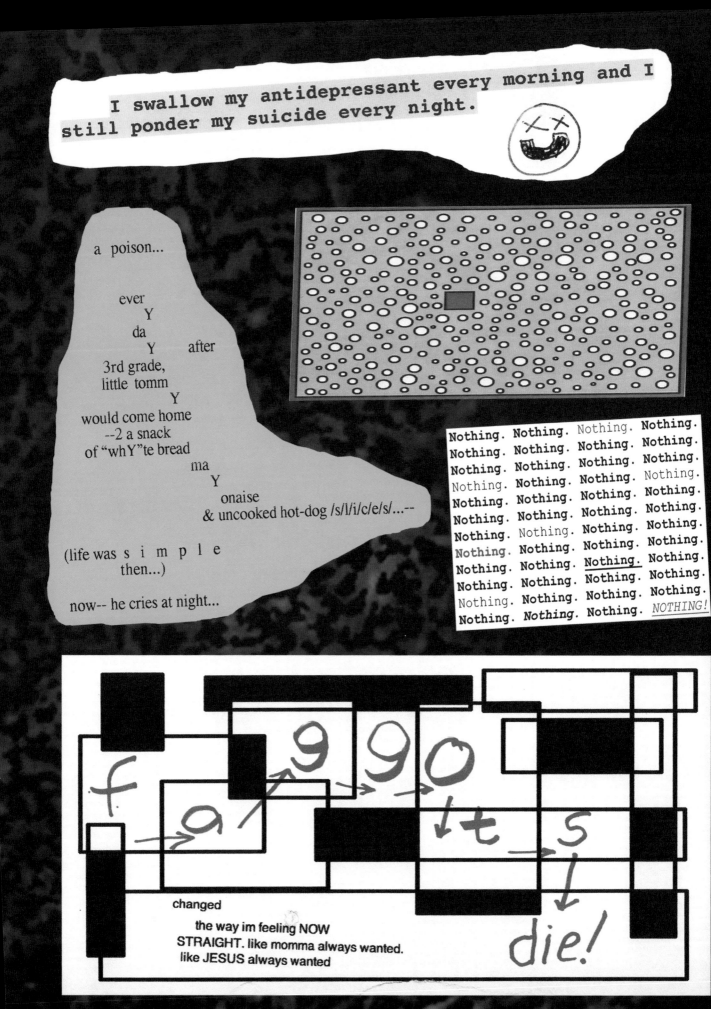

I swallow my antidepressant every morning and I still ponder my suicide every night.

a poison...

everY
daY after
3rd grade,
little tommY
would come home
--2 a snack
of "whY"te bread
maY
onaise
& uncooked hot-dog /s/l/i/c/e/s/...--

(life was s i m p l e
then...)

now-- he cries at night...

Nothing. Nothing. Nothing. Nothing.
Nothing. Nothing. Nothing. Nothing.
Nothing. Nothing. Nothing. Nothing.
Nothing. Nothing. Nothing. Nothing.
Nothing. Nothing. Nothing. Nothing.
Nothing. Nothing. Nothing. Nothing.
Nothing. Nothing. Nothing. Nothing.
Nothing. Nothing. Nothing. Nothing.
Nothing. Nothing. Nothing. Nothing.
Nothing. Nothing. Nothing. Nothing.
Nothing. Nothing. Nothing. Nothing.
Nothing. Nothing. Nothing. NOTHING!

f. a 9 9 0 It s die!

changed
the way im feeling NOW
STRAIGHT. like momma always wanted.
like JESUS always wanted

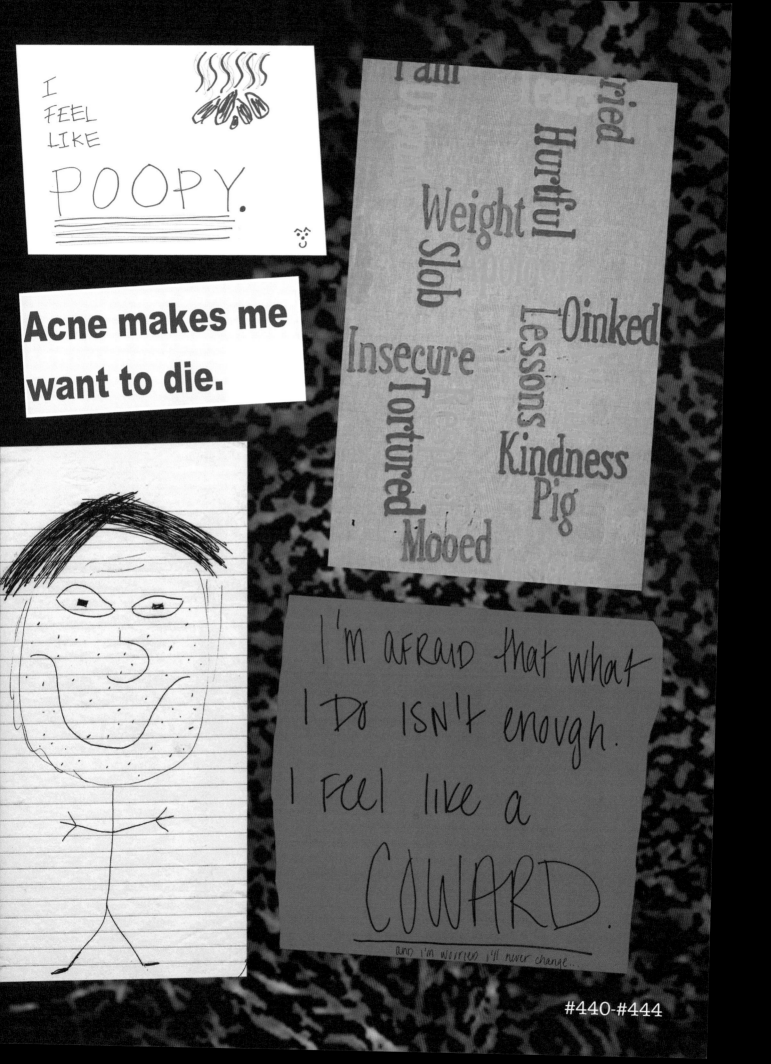

My life has become:

- Laundry
- Burping a baby who I think hates me
- Walking a cat (yes!!!)
- Attempting to lose 40 pounds that just won't fall off
- Watching daytime TV
- Walking to the bus stop twice a day
- Making Kraft mac-n-cheese
- Keeping my hair short because "It's just so much easier."
- The constant Giving of myself with a painted on ☺
- Watching crappy cartoons on repeat
- Chauffeuring around
- Constantly denying that I AM NOT my mother
- Pretending to be a kid soccer fan
- Pretending to be MOM soccer fan (I HATE THEM ALL!)
- Wine. WIne. WINe. WINE. WINE! WINE!!!!!
- Planning over-priced trips to Florida that my children do not deserve
- Fake laughing at the jokes of a man who pretends to love me (I think he pretends. I cannot tell anymore.)

I despise your enchanting eyes. They've changed my life. I no longer have excuses.

You've forced me to grow up. People say that I'm the strong one. They often ask me how I can stay with someone as quiet as you. My mother thinks you have no personality and our daughter thinks you're boring. But unlike them, I knew you WHEN.

The 80's! WHEN you used to ride a motorcycle and give my father the finger and punch any guy that disrespected me. Do you even know how much that used to turn me on?

Now you're a good father, good husband, good man. The motorcycle is gone and you keep your hands to yourself. You let me shine when we're out showing off in the world. You've mellowed and asked me to step up as matriarch. I have tried. Are you proud of me?

All I ask is that when Laura and Bill grow up and leave for college that you buy back that bike, tell my dad to "Fuck Off!!!" and punch out any man who doesn't worship me like you do.

I am your queen and you are my king. We're going to make it.

#609

I FEEL VERY BLESSED TO HAVE A VERY WONDERFUL LIFE. MY KIDS AND I SHARE A "COZY" 1 BEDROOM APARTMENT WHICH KEEPS US VERY CLOSE WITH EACH OTHER LITERALLY AND FIGURATIVELY. WE DON'T HAVE A LOT OF MONEY BUT WE ARE RICH IN THE THINGS THAT TRULY MATTER - LOVE, SUPPORT, ATTENTION AND CARING. ALL OF THE THINGS THAT I DID NOT HAVE GROWING UP.

MY HOME LIFE WAS PHYSICALLY, MENTALLY AND EMOTIONALLY ABUSIVE. I NEVER UNDERSTOOD WHY. WHEN I WAS 14 I WAS WITHIN SECONDS OF SLASHING MY WRISTS BECAUSE I JUST WANTED IT TO STOP! THE ONLY REASON THAT I DIDN'T WAS BECAUSE A TEACHER HAD GIVEN ME HIS PHONE NUMBER AND A QUARTER AND SAID THAT IF I EVER NEEDED ANYTHING TO CALL. I DIDN'T CALL BUT THE GESTURE SAVED MY LIFE.

TODAY I AM A HAPPY, WELL ADJUSTED, PROUD MOM OF 2 TEENAGERS.

BE "THE" LOVE !

#700

When I was a freshmen in College I was ripped from My secure cocky rich boy self and forced to grow up in a matter of months. I'm a type 1 diabetic but it didn't get bad until ~~I~~ I started to go through the pledgeship experience. I was accepted into the most respected frat on campus where they really do make you go through hell for 8 months to actually be a part of this organization. After many beatings, diabetic hospitalizations and dropped classes. I left the frat and the school. I went back home to the security of my family but it wasn't there. My father had enough of my spoiled antics and he failed to realize that I was truly hurt. He told me I was a pussy, that he didn't love me and to leave. I didn't know ~~tell~~ what to do. In a matter of 2 months. My girlfriend cheated on me, she got pregnant. and had an abortion. I was washing windows for a living and coming home to a alcohol filled fridge and a single bed in an apartment with nothing Else. One night I literally prayed for God to end my life. He didn't instead things slowly got better over the next 5 years. That experience shaped me as a human. If I had checked out early I wouldn't have a beautiful fiance. A wonderful relationship with my father and a ~~growing~~ growing acting career that I love. I love my life because ~~one even I went through~~

#770

Right now I'm thinking..... about the other night when I slept over at my grandma's house. My younger sister & I were laying in bed talking like we usually do. We talked about school. I love hearing all the drama that takes place in the 4th grade! We also talked about my resent break-up & all the boys she said she liked, But then she started crying & at first I was annoyed like come on its late and why the hell you crying.?! She told me I won't understand right then but she tell me when she's older. I was a little confused like what could she be talking about, tell me when she's older what would that matter, Evenally I got her to tell me... She had said that she lied about likeing the boys in her class that she didn't like boys at all. I was shoked & a little hurt that she didn't wanna tell me this that she though I wouldn't understand her. I told her about me being in love with my best friend Sam for years and I know how it is to feel different and how it feel like what you are is wrong but its not its who she is and I still love her I even love her a little more to trust me with herself like that!

my biggest fear? death. or loss. I am afraid of losing my dad to alcoholism. we tried to tell him, but that was the last string to the divorce. with his father dying when he was fifty two from alcoholism, I fear I will lose my dad too. my dad turned 52 in July. I just want to make him happy and proud but nothing seems good enough anymore. I fear he won't be here to walk me down the aisle at my wedding. I have always been daddy's little girl. I can't seem to bare the thought of losing him from me. Calling him past 10:00 anymore is useless considering he is usually hammered. why can't he just get help and stop blamming my mom. I want a happy family like other people.

From the Artist: "This is one of the first media art pieces I ever made. I call it 'Falling Maternal'. For a long time, I hated my mother for reasons I care not to explain. All I'll say is she said something that no mother should say to a child...but when I fell apart, and realized that her warnings were correct, she was the only person there to catch me as my world crumbled. She didn't say 'I told you so!' She didn't forsake me like everyone else. She didn't let my disease define me. She told me I was beautiful...She stayed with me when no one else would...We may not see eye to eye, but we've learned to meet somewhere in the middle. That is all I ever wanted."

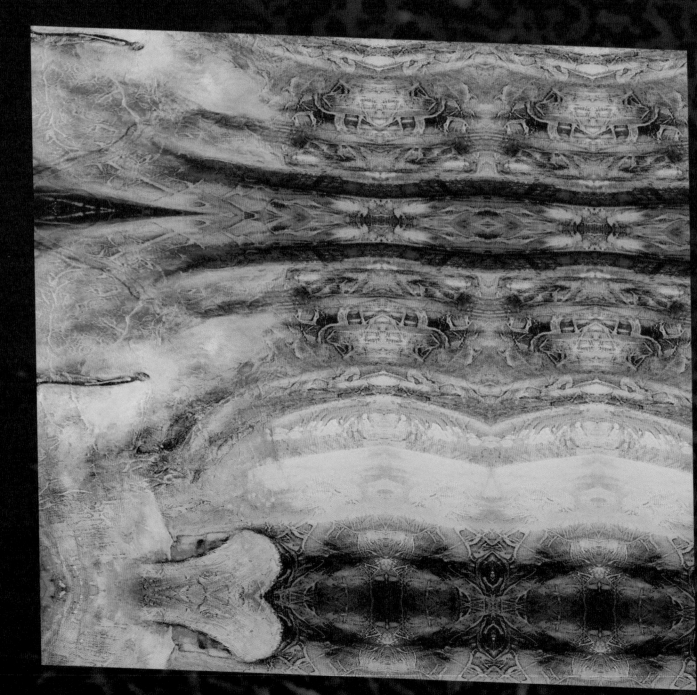

#034

My aunt - my very favorite aunt
- took her own life.
And nothing in the world -
not children, not husband,
not money, not art...
not a million blessings in
my life
have been enough to fill
the empty spot she left in
my heart.
You see, when you loose
someone who loved you so much,
you live with a hole in your
heart, forever!

Entitled: "On the Street
Where She Lived"

Entitled: "Based on a
Poem about Mother"

#047-#049

Waiting - I am always waiting. I've worked so hard to get to where I am now. Now I am on the edge of a cliff, the wind is rushing into my wings. All I have to do now is jump, and it's the only thing I cannot bring myself together to do. I wanted someone. I wanted her to be miserable. I learned quickly that anyone can do anything as long as he knows that someone is worse off then he is. What I was not expecting was learning when that someone worse off is someone you love, the catharsis multiplies exponentially. I wanted her to stay, and make my hesitation look normal. Now I am alone. Now I will be forced to succeed. Maybe this was the reason people wanted a rapture. A chance to escape. A chance to see + experience something new. Even if we all die, for one brief moment we experience as a people something that no one has ever seen before. Humans are strange people. At once we want to be noticed, and to be completely anonymous. We want identity. We want alter-egos.

I feel like I'm an assassin, like I'm Hercules. Like I've been sent here to kill all of you. To kill all of your dreams, to stifle all your creativity, to make you succumb to all the pressures you may feel to the point that you have absolutely no oxygen left to breath out of that pathetic little opening you call a mouth. I will beat you, defeat you and make you wish you had n7ever ever attempted to even think for one second that you could compete with me. You do not have the right to be in the same room as me. You have no pedigree, no prerequisites, no referrals. You are as worthless as meat to a vegetarian. You have been weighed, your value has been quantified and you will always fall short. Not because you didn't try hard enough, not because you didn't do everything in your power to make it happen. It's because at the end of the day, you never had, I.T. You are inadequate. Please just accept this fate.

— Success

#207

Comfort in monotony.

She stands in line at the McDonald's.
Outside the snow falls.
Families monopolize the streets, Christmas shopping.
(Only three days left, you know.)
It's the most commercial time of the year!
Yet, she is alone.

A story is written in her soft eyes.
They say her name is Helen... Or Cheryl.
She wears a beige trench coat, tightly secured around her waist.
Which is accompanied by a too teal scarf.
Her blonde-in-a-box hair shows her envious quest for youth.
Fashionable at forty.

Probably on her way home from the train station.
After a hard day in her downtown office.
An accountant, no doubt.

She orders a Fish Fillet sandwich.
As she does every Tuesday night.
In her hand, she holds the latest Danielle Steel novel.
It keeps her company on these hectic, winter nights.
No one else will.

All she wants is a smile.
All she needs is a kind word.

She makes her way to a table for two.
As she sits, she mindlessly unwraps her death-on-a-bun and opens her paperback.
Her bookmark says she is on page 127.
But, in bitter reality, she's only on 33.
"Always look busy," Mom used to say.

A father asks if he can borrow her extra chair.
He is unaware of the damage he has done.
But, she has no objection.
No use for it.
The story of her life.

Outside, the snow continues to fall.
With no two snowflakes exactly alike.

#168

Dear G,

I feel trapped. I feel that no matter what I end up doing the sacrifice would be too big and ~~the~~ pain too much to bear.

I miss my mom. I miss my dad. Grandma. my brother. But at the same time I want it so bad. I think of all the missed opportunities and the pain becomes paralyzing, knowing that I could've had it all by now.

I don't enjoy my life. I don't like it. And knowing that the window is about to close only adds to my feeling of desperation and despair.

I need your help. I will not stop trying regardless of whether the situation gets better, ~~may~~ just because there is nothing else out there for me. But please help me, because I really feel like I can't take it anymore.

will always remember prom - 06/2010 - 06-2011

#725

Are my parents still considering divorce? How is my guinea pig getting along with my new cat? What is my orientation? Will I finish my book report? Why is my crayon box all smashed? I wish I could get my room clean. Animaniacs was a great show, they shouldn't have canceled it. My pencil is too dull. Does my sister have lice? Am I doing this right? Is Michelle okay? I like TIME. I'm hungry and want some taquitos.

thought thought thought thought thought thought thought thought thought thought thought thought thought thought thought thought

me me me me me me me me me me hair hair hair hair hair hair hair me me me me me me

me me me me me me shirt shirt shirt shirt shirt shirt shirt me me me me me me

desk desk desk desk desk desk desk desk desk desk desk

Restroom Reflections.

Ruth removed the backpack from her shoulders and set it on the counter of the restroom sink. She was glad that the book store's three stalled room was empty. Although it was a typical Tuesday night in December, the young woman felt anything but typical. She felt sick. Sick to her stomach. As if it were instinct, she pulled a brush from one of the bag's oversized pockets and began to run it through her hair. She looked into the mirror.

What if he doesn't like me? Oh, God... I'm being so stupid. He doesn't have to like me. Coffee. It's coffee... But, it's coffee with him. Oh God...

She took a plastic clip from her backpack, pulled her hair half up, and fastened it into place. She knew he liked it that way. Religiously, he had always told her when her hair looked nice. He called her his "Greek Goddess." Her supple, tanned skin and flowing dark hair made the title believable. Her penetrating, green eyes and stately profile completed the classic facial ensemble. Simply put, she was a mother's dream daughter. A seventeen-year-old at a cut above the rest. A member of the school's honor society. A volunteer at the local nursing home and soup kitchen. A gifted writer and talented musician. Ruth was perfect enough to hate yet loved by all. People were drawn to her uniquely optimistic outlook. Her special sense of being. Unlike other beautiful, teenage girls, she was approachable. Something in the girl's demeanor seemed to give away her outgoing and ever-giving personality. In short, Ruth was the girl next door that had it all...

...Until I lost him.

She checked herself one last time. Her eyes looked a little heavy, but there was nothing she could do about that. Besides, what teenage girl did get enough sleep? She had so many important things on her mind.

AP English... Play practice... Those damn college applications... Him. Besides, seeing him was about as good as dreaming. Has it really been six months? Six months?

The unnaturally nerved teen smiled one last time in the mirror. She checked her teeth for lipstick, dropped her brush back into its designated compartment, and made her way to the door. Before leaving, though, she looked out empty room's skylight. She could see snow collecting on the domed glass. The first snow of the year. Snow always reminded Ruth of him.

Everyone has that special someone. That first love that you can never seem to shake. He's the guy that my mind always drifts back to when I'm talking a midsummer night's walk or sitting by a fire... Or watching the snow fall from my bedroom window. He's like the snow. From the security of my heated bedroom, it looks so peaceful and inviting. I want to touch it. I yearn to touch it. However, I know that if I was out there, the biting cold would pierce me to the core. I'd wish I was in my bedroom again. He's like the snow... And, with his warm, contradictory touch, I inevitably melt away too.

Ruth shook her head and threw her backpack over her left shoulder. She began to reaffirm to herself by outlining the evening's rules.

There will be no more comparing him to anything. No more organic metaphors or figurative meanings or motifs. No more AP English crap. Not tonight, Ruth. Not tonight.

Ruth grabbed the handle of the bathroom door. She took a deep breath and opened it. The burning sensation in her chest almost seemed to contradict the coldness of the brass handle. She stepped into the holiday business of the book store, wondering if the fluorescent lighting made her look bad. Bad enough for him to walk away. Again.

From the Author: "This is a short story I wrote when I was 16 years old. 16 years later, and it is exactly the same way I feel each time I see the ex-love of my life...Soulmates do exist."

Whenever I am asked to reflect about how I am feeling, I am transported back to a moment three years ago. It was the day my boyfriend returned home and told me he was leaving me (At first he said it was because he no longer loved me, but he later admitted that it was because he found someone more vibrant. Yes, he used the words "more vibrant".)

I must have looked like an idiot. I was on my knees begging him to stay with me. With no emotion, he was packing his suitcase and with all the emotion in the world, I was screaming for him to change his mind. I got nothing out of him, so I began to use the tactics that I was taught in theatre school. They always told us that if at first your character doesn't succeed, try attacking the problem from a different point of view.

So I tried everything. I insulted him, I made fun of him, I tried the silent treatment, I helped him pack, I cried louder, I cried softer, I threatened to kill myself, I threatened to kill him, I threatened to give our dog away. Nothing changed his mind. Whoever this "more vibrant" person was had a real hold over him. He was going to leave no matter what I did.

So instead I asked him for one thing. I wanted a last memory of the two of us together that I could always remember. I leaned in to kiss him, but he jerked away. I told him I needed something from him, so he threw a t-shirt at me. He coldly said, "Have it! There's your memory!"

I knew it would be pathetic of me to take it, so I told him, "Fuck you!" (Secretly however I tucked the shirt away in my nightstand so I would always have it.) I knew things were over. He finished packing and left my apartment. We were together for 27 months and that was the last time I ever saw him. Not only did he leave me for someone more vibrant, but he moved across the country to be with this more vibrant person. I've never met this person and probably never will but They are still together, so maybe it was meant to be. He has true love, and I have his tshirt.

It no longer smells like him. For a few weeks, I wore it when I was alone. I only put it on after I took a shower. I wanted to be as clean as possible so my smells did not get in its fiber and infect it. I didn't want the memories in his t-shirt to be lost. (I love the way he smells, but I hate the way I smell.)

Over time, though, my smell took over and now I have this old white shirt that smells like me. All the stains on it are stains I put on it. I spilled coffee wearing it one morning. There's a grass stain and a blue pen mark. He gave me a pristine white t-shirt that smelled so beautiful and sweet and I turned it into something dirty and reeking of self-hate. I tell myself I should throw it away, but I know I never will. so I tell myself to wash it, but that would be like burning his memory out of the shirt. So I just leave it balled up in the back of my closet. It shares a space with a few other memories from other exes that I've liked then loved then lost. His t-shirt however is the most special of the bunch.

Sadly, if there was a fire in my apartment, it is probably the first and only thing I'd take with me. I'd let the past burn away, but I'd save that t-shirt. Part of me thinks that it's romantic and part of me thinks that it is pathetic but all of misses him at least once a day.

I wish I was more vibrant.

head pounding, knees shacking
whole body acheing, will I
ever want to walk again?
feel as if the world will
never let me rest, cause of
one pactice 2 up & down
the stairs ~~ago~~ I go,
along with my heart &
soul. both asking for forgiveness
yet receive none, for my heart
won't stop loving the wrong ones,
my soul living for my love one, and
my body dying from 2 much fun.
how is it ~~th~~ my, heart, body & soul
hurt? yet I don't know which ones
worst... Cause my body will heal
from all the damage it's taken, & my
heart will heal all the pain its concealed,
and my ~~heart~~ will live even after my
love won't give. But in the end is it
worth it? Cause I am left with a
body that seems to suffocate, a heart
that just won't stop beating to your
name, and a soul that will live, but
has no life. Cause u left me bleeding,

I still love you... yes I do... but
moving on is my plan ~~a~~ too. I was not
chosen I was left behind, but I have faith
that some one can make my life shine.
~~also I~~ Also, I hope I can be with this
person for a life time... sorry greg

#603

Chords progress. Music swells. The melody dances with my emotions. I'm slightly drunk. Only two beers in. However two beers are enough to get me to lay down the front and open up the flood gates. It's a house party. The lights are on and no parents are home.

She is a beautiful girl. No, a beautiful woman. At 17 she already defines grace and does not yet know that she does so. I don't think she'll ever understand this. Her inability to see herself as perfect is one of her charms.

I love her. She empowers me. Yet we both live in boxes and it will never be more than it is. Two newly discovered best friends drinking beer and laughing about the fucktard who just threw up in the hot tub.

She is broken. Dumped by a jock after what can only be described as a forced parental abortion. I am gay and out and proud. We connect in a way I've never connected with a woman before. It's the same way I've connected with other boys.

I don't want to date her. I don't even want to kiss her. I just wish we didn't live in a world that put us in such boxes. Life continually forks the road, but labels and definitions force us to take the road that most travel.

If we continue taking the roads most traveled, trail blazers will cease to exist.

I'm not saying I am straight or that she could "turn" me. I love being a gay queer boy. She just stirs something in me, and I wish I could express that without freaking out all of the friends and family who have worked so hard to accept me.

She's a person needing. I'm a person "feeling". Why can't we connect even in the most non-sexual of ways?

Mostly though. I wish we weren't put into boxes for her sake. Everyone looks at her as broken, slutty, scarred, used, damaged, worthless. They've shoved instruments inside her and removed a growing life.

She smiles at me from across the room. It is genuine and filled with hope but also apprehension. I know if I told her how I felt, it would change nothing and yet would change everything. To have someone tell you that you are beautiful even when it doesn't make sense........I don't know.

I want to heal her. I want her to see what I see.

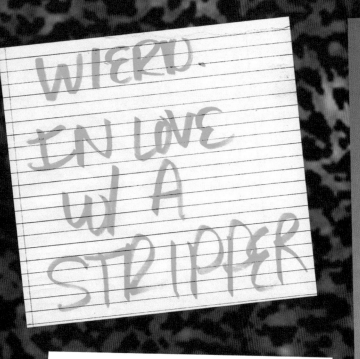

HO

RNY

From the Artist: "This is my 'Dream Woman'. I am still waiting on her...one day, hopefully."

My friend. My life. My "boyfriend". My Billy R.
You say I hurt you, but I never ~~di~~ realized
what you actually meant. You suffered after
you broke up with me, and I had no idea.
You helped me through my depression, the hardest
time in my life. I know I can talk to you
about anything, and all i want is for me to
be that person for you. I want to be as important
to you as you are to me. When I see you at
school, my heart drops. skips a beat. I JUST WANT
TO BE YOURS AGAIN. let me back. We both know
that we grew apart, and you made the right
decision at the time. don't regret doing it. We
will have our time again and we will know
how to do it right this time. I love you.

never forget it.

(_____me_____) is fairly convinced that I will die alone with 47 cats and 00000 memories of what it feels like to be loved (I mean, really and truly loved) by a man.

I am convinced.

I Remember Me... ~~about~~ Dont forget Me...

In the morning I wake up, with out a thought... wondering how my day would be... hopefully just you & me. I know you left, and I'm left behind a Feeling lonely & forgotten. All I have is your text messages. I always wait for the weekend where we will see each other once again. See, it goes a little something like this. You walked into my life, not knowing how much you would change it, You walked into my little world... and the same goes to my heart. as i miss you, I cant wait till the day I see you... ONCE AGAIN. YOU, YOU, left with me letters you know i fell in love with you. YOU, YOU, YOU, YOU, YOU, YOU, YOU, YOU, YOU, YOU, is all i think about... I miss you, i miss you,

Thank you for waking into my life. & promising to stay there no matter where life TAKES US.

Dont Forget Me, bcuz i'll always Remember you...

FaceFaceFaceFace
face i love your eyes
face moon and eyes
way leves face & face

He turns water into wine and He raises the dead back to life.

Maybe that's why I'm an alcoholic who feels dead inside.

He works miracles and He will fix me if I pray just a little bit harder.

I know this is true.

Is it wrong that I think images of Jesus on the cross are sexy? ☺ ☺ ☺ ☺ ☺ ☺ ☺ ☺ ☺ ☺ ☺ ☺

Dear God, Fuck You!!!!! ♥, a slut

I think the point of life is worshiping Allah the only God there is no God but Him. God is the Creator of the whole world starting with Adam and Eve till now. He created you, me, and everyone. He created us to worship Him. And if we made the right choice we will go to Genna the place that is so Great that no eye have seen and no ear have heard about. You should try this point of view you will be happy when u find the truth.

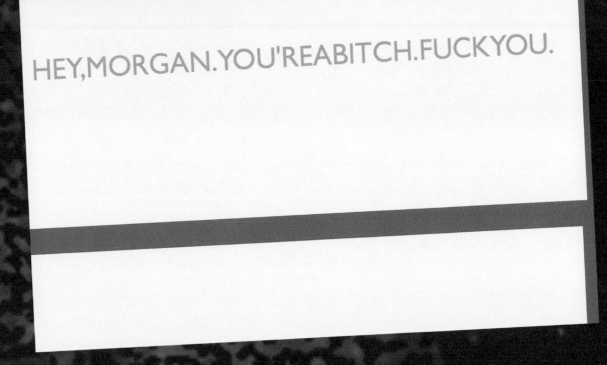

HEY,MORGAN.YOU'REABITCH.FUCKYOU.

Entitled by Artists: "Two paintings by two artists who just happen to be boyfriend and girlfriend who just happened to be named Tommy and Morgan and who share a studio apartment and are on the verge of breaking up." Or: "We know these paintings suck but we have given up and you can go fuck yourself." Or: "On Canvas, $49 cash."

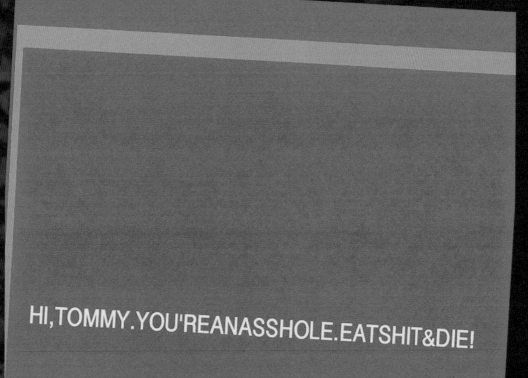

HI,TOMMY.YOU'REANASSHOLE.EATSHIT&DIE!

Every single day Im asked how I feel today I often say im good or okay but truth is im not even close to that okay. right now I feel upset, their is no words I can say to explain how Im feeling deep inside, my tears wont help me feel better and each day that goes by feels longer; millions of smiles on the hallway but one frown that's me im the frown. I guess things haven't been the same ever since he left before I use to love walking up in the morning I use to love getting outta bed on cold winter nights I use to love going to school I use to love me. I remember all our moments all those special sparkles, his eyes that couldn't take his eyes off me and I remember that special feeling when he would say my name or hug me. This year his gone he's not here no more I cant lie I miss him and I been misrable ever since he left, I find my self not concentrating anymore not caring about anything not even life. My best friend wont even look at me with all these arguments and all these fighting the silence hurts me more not talking to both of them has killed me Im surprised I had let my self made it this far. At the end of the day the only person you can really count on is youre self, but what if not even youre self wants to help you anymore. My back is against the wall my heart is broken completly it's like I have no air and I am slowly painfully dieing I want my life back, I want my best friend back I want him back Life just hasn't been good the same </3

– All alone

Right now...I feel tired. Not so much physically, as emotionally. This is my third flight in five days, and the circulated airplane air always seems to exhaust my emotions. I always thought this is what I wanted, to travel for living. In 2010 alone, I've zip-lined my way through the Alaskan rainforest, climbed the volcanoes of Santorini, got into a bar fight in Nashville (!!!), slept on the beach in Xtapa and stood at Ground Zero - crying for hours, why I do not know. Traveling, experiencing, writing about it and getting paid; I thought that's what I wanted - the coveted job title of "internationally published travel writer".

Now, I feel like George Clooney in that movie: me, my iPod and my suitcase - electronic emptiness.

To say that I'm alone would be a dramatic overstatement. I have a boyfriend...a "life partner". I feel cared for. I feel that, when/if push comes/came to shove, I'd have someone there to take care of me - visit me in the hospital, bail me out of jail, accompany me to my mother's funeral, be there for me whatever way the wind blows. I do not, however, feel loved.

We have not touched in years - literally, not touched. Not a single kiss. We still sleep in the same bed. But sometimes I feel his leg brush against mine and then he violently jerks away. I playfully rub his knee, and I feel his entire body tense. I give him a hug, and he simply goes limp. He is my partner - but not my boyfriend, mate or lover. Not my yang. Not my salvation.

I find some comfort in knowing that I'll never be alone. And yet I ache with the pathetic emptiness this "partnership" breeds in my soul. The deepest parts of me wonder - Am I not good enough? Am I ugly? Do I even deserve to be held, kissed, romanced, caressed, made love to? I believe all those things are human rights - things that every person deserves. Every person...except for me.

I stare out this airplane window, watching the sun as it breaks the horizon. The world is so big, so beautiful, filled with so many people - so how can I feel this alone...?

A Million Pieces (or not)

Once upon a time, a guy wrote a novel called *A Million Little Pieces* and that is always how I described my emotional state. I always told people that I was "breaking into a million little pieces". Then we realized that book was mostly fake and I realized that I was just super dramatic.

Pieces of you can chip off but we can never shatter upon a single impact into a million pieces. People are like a marble that is centuries old. Humans have survived the test of time. We shall overcome and endure.

We do not break into "a million little pieces." Chips occasionally flake off, but it only reveals our true selves that lie beneath. Waiting to be uncovered and dying to be released.